GOLF QUIZ

GOLF QUIZ

BY HERBERT WARREN WIND

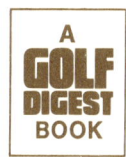

Copyright© 1975, 1976, 1977, 1978, 1979,
1980 by Golf Digest/Tennis Inc.
All rights reserved including the
right of reproduction in whole or in
part in any form.

Published by Golf Digest/Tennis Inc.,
A New York Times Company,
495 Westport Avenue
Norwalk, Connecticut 06856

Trade book distribution by
Simon and Schuster
A Division of Gulf & Western Corporation,
New York, New York 10020

First Printing
ISBN: 0-914178-41-5
Library of Congress: 80-66690
Manufactured in the United
States of America

Cover and book design by Dorothy Geiser.
Typesetting by Intercontinental Publications,
Westport, Conn.
Printing and binding by R.R. Donnelley & Sons.

CREDITS:

ILLUSTRATION:
Newcomb, John, 12, 34, 89, 120, 150, 173, 196, 223, 224, 246
Okamoto, Mona, 20, 64, 102, 114, 162, 210

PHOTOGRAPHY:
United States Golf Association, 16, 24, 44, 126, 176
United Press International, 36, 82, 112, 164, 190
Hertzberg, Will, 42, 182
Lacey, E.D., 46
Curtis, Bruce, 48
M. Silver Associates, 66
Shell Photo by Power, Hal, 70
Hemmer, John, 73
Associated Press, 80
Atlanta Journal, 96
Newcomb, John, 106, 228
Szurlej, Steve, 116, 134, 186A, 186B, 214
May, J.P., 140
Chritton, Michael, 240
Romero, Bill, 244

FOREWORD

While it is always a great thrill just to be on the premises when a major golf title is being contested, one fringe benefit I particularly enjoy is the chance to run into and chat with Herbert Warren Wind.

Herb, who writes long and masterful accounts of the action at the Masters, U.S. and British Opens and PGA Championship for *The New Yorker,* is a delightful conversationalist and a golf raconteur of the first order. As he

PGA Commissioner Deane Beman, Herb Wind and Golf Digest editor Nick Seitz exchanging golf trivia at a recent Masters bash.

has demonstrated in numerous books over the years, most particularly in his monumental *The Story of American Golf* (Knopf, 1975), he has an encyclopedic grasp on the events, personalities and issues that have gone into the history of the game. And naturally he is great to have around the press tent at places like Augusta National when facts or figures about some great match or tournament of the past slip the mind.

One year Herb confessed to me a weakness for re-cycling some of the golf trivia he knows in the form of multiple-choice questions for his friends. I urged him to go public with his game by composing an entire exam's worth of the questions for the readers of *Golf Digest*. Herb has written thoughtful pieces for us on large themes such as golf architecture and the evolution of the game in this country, but here was something he—and our readers—could have fun with. And so was born "Herbert Warren Wind's Golf Quiz." It is now a fixture in our February annual recordbook issue every year, and at the rate Herb keeps coming up with interesting and amusing stumpers, it is likely to remain a fixture for a long time to come.

I am delighted to see the first six quizzes collected, and so entertainingly illustrated, here.

Nick Seitz
Editor, *Golf Digest*

1 Only one of these statements about Ben Hogan is not true. Can you isolate it?

   A. He did not win a major championship until 1946 when he defeated Ed Oliver in the finals of the PGA Championship.

   B. His famous remark, "I am glad I brought this monster to its knees," was made at the presentation ceremony at Oakland Hills on which he had just won the 1951 U.S. Open.

   C. In winning the 1967 Masters, his third and last triumph in that tournament, he played the second nine in 30 strokes on the third round, and it proved to be the key to his victory.

   D. His epochal triumph in the 1953 British Open was scored at Carnoustie and was exceptional in that he bettered his score round by round: 73-71-70-68.

10 GOLF QUIZ

 Hogan did play the third round of the 1967 Masters in 36-30-66, but did not win the tournament. He won two Masters, in 1951 and 1953.

2 When the USGA prepares a course for the Open championship, the fairways are bordered by

A. A strip of "secondary rough" about two inches high and then by "primary rough" roughly between four and six inches high.
B. A uniform growth of rough 10 inches high.
C. A strip of five-inch rough, a strip of 10-inch rough and finally a strip of 15-inch rough.
D. A belt of Bermuda grass, a belt of gorse and bracken and finally a punishing belt of opium poppies and poison hemlock.

12 GOLF QUIZ

A. Notwithstanding, sometimes the rough seems as rugged as D.

GOLF QUIZ 13

3 Only one of these statements is correct:

A. Willie Macfarlane played his last stroke on the 72nd hole, the one that earned him a tie in the 1925 U.S. Open, with a mid-iron.

B. When Arnold Palmer won the 1960 U.S. Open at Cherry Hills, he did it by uncorking a tremendous charge of six birdies on the last seven holes.

C. Ken Venturi still managed to win the 1964 U.S. Open despite the fact that, nearing heat exhaustion, he finished with a bogey and a double bogey.

D. In the colorful 1972 Open at Pebble Beach, Jack Nicklaus' margin of victory rested on the great 1-iron he played to the 71st which landed a foot from the hole, hit the flagstick, and left him a tap-in birdie putt.

A. Macfarlane's approach putt finished in a depression in the green two feet or so from the hole. He noticed this when he had to mark his ball since it was in the line of his playing partner. After replacing it, he chose to hole out with his midiron, feeling it was safer under the circumstances than the putter.

4 Carolyn Cudone made history in 1972 when she became

A. The first player to win the U.S. Girls' Junior Championship three consecutive years.

B. The sixth American to carry off the British Ladies' Championship.

C. The first golfer ever to win a U.S. national championship five years in a row.

D. The first amateur since JoAnne Gunderson to capture an LPGA event.

16 GOLF QUIZ

C. No man or woman has won a U.S. Open or Amateur more than three straight times. The same is true of all the other national championships conducted by the USGA, except for the Women's Senior in which Mrs. Cudone had her streak. Walter Hagen, however, won the PGA Championship four straight years, 1924–1927.

5 In the following list, there are four groups of three items. In only one instance the three items are not a legitimate part of the same category. The incorrect trio is

A. Iron Man, Rabbit Dyer, Tip Anderson.
B. Pebble Beach, Del Monte Hills, Cypress Point.
C. Rae's Creek, Swilken Burn, Baffling Brook.
D. Harry Vardon, J.H. Taylor, James Braid.

18 GOLF QUIZ

B. There is no course on the Monterey Peninsula called Del Monte Hills. The Crosby uses three courses on the peninsula: Pebble Beach, Cypress Point, and Spyglass Hill. Before Spyglass was built, the tournament used the Monterey Country Club, which is also on the peninsula, as its third course. (A is made up of three caddies, C of three water hazards, at the Augusta National, St. Andrews and Merion, respectively, and D of the three golfers who formed The Triumvirate in Britain shortly after the turn of the century.)

6. The "Amen Corner" has become accepted vernacular to describe

A. The 6th, 7th and 8th holes at Pebble Beach.
B. The 11th, 12th and 13th holes at the Augusta National.
C. The 7th, 8th, 9th, 10th and 11th holes at St. Andrews.
D. The 11th and 12th holes at Merion.

20 GOLF QUIZ

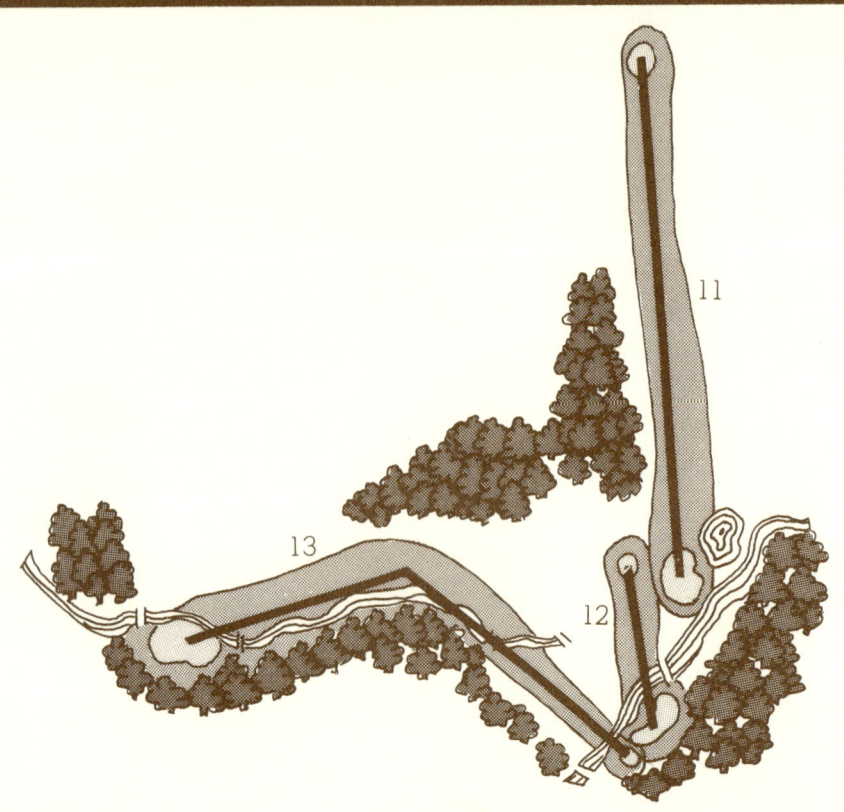

B. Rae's Creek is very much in prominence on these three holes.

7 Robert Tyre Jones Jr. attended the following three institutions of learning:

A. Georgia, Georgia Tech and Sewanee Law.
B. Georgia Tech, Harvard and Emory Law.
C. Georgia, Oxford and Harvard Law.
D. Washington & Lee, St. Andrews and Virginia Law.

22 GOLF QUIZ

Jones never graduated from Emory Law, however, for he passed the Georgia state bar exams midway during his second year.

8 Who was the man who won the U.S. Open in 1937 and 1938, the Masters in 1939, the Western Open in 1936, 1937 and 1938, and then, suddenly and mysteriously, lost his swing and with it his ability to play winning golf?

A. Ky Laffoon.
B. Macdonald Smith.
C. Leo Diegel.
D. Ralph Guldahl.

D. There have been few strokeplay masters in his class.

9 Sam Snead keeps rolling on forever. He was never more remarkable than in winning the PGA Seniors Championship in 1973 with the following scores:

A. 70-70-70-70–280, eight under par.
B. 67-70-69-71–277, eleven under par.
C. 66-66-67-69–268, twenty under par.
D. 72-70-70-66–278, ten under par.

26 GOLF QUIZ

 And he missed a few putts he might well have made.

GOLF QUIZ 27

10 The late Charley Bartlett of the Chicago Tribune made it a particular point to learn the middle names of prominent golfers. He would have known that among the quartet of stars listed below only one of the four names is incorrect.

A. Lee Buck Trevino.
B. Arnold David Palmer.
C. Albert Winsborough Yancey.
D. Jack William Nicklaus.

28 GOLF QUIZ

 Arnold's middle name is Daniel.

11 Before the wooden tee was invented, to facilitate hitting a good tee shot, golfers customarily

    A. Used a plastic tee.
    B. Clipped a small piece of turf with their niblick from the area around the tee and simply set their ball up on that.
    C. Placed their ball in the small concave hollow at the top of a piece of sponge rubber that was shaped roughly like a pyramid.
    D. Took a pinch of sand from the so-called tee-box, wet it with water from a pail in the tee-box and built a sand tee for the ball with their fingers.

30 GOLF QUIZ

—from *The Game of Golf*, by Willie Park, Jr., published 1896

D. Tee-boxes vanished after the 1920s.

12 It is a par 3 only 120 yards or so in length. You hit down to a small green from an elevated tee. The green is practically surrounded by bunkers, and, for good measure, the spray from the pounding ocean often provides a beautiful if alarming backdrop. It is:

A. The seventh at Pebble Beach.
B. The 17th at Pebble Beach.
C. The 15th at Cypress Point.
D. The 16th at Cypress Point.

32 GOLF QUIZ

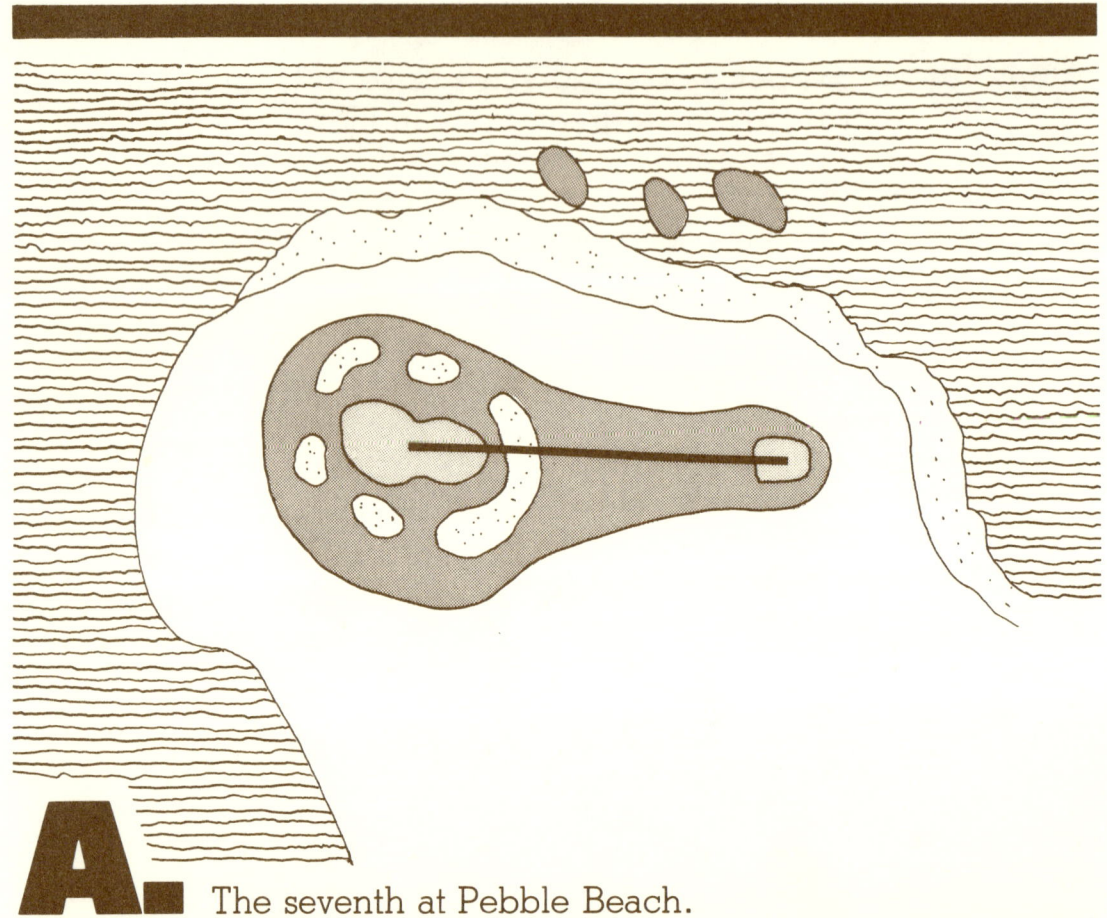

A. The seventh at Pebble Beach.

13 According to the Rules of Golf, if you are playing in a competition and looking for a lost ball

A. You are allotted five minutes in which to find it.

B. You can look for it for "eight minutes maximum" provided you wave through any group of players you would otherwise be holding up.

C. Under the new rules to speed up play, you have "three minutes only to locate the ball, after which the contestant must duly proceed with the playing of his round."

D. You are permitted to search the area "for a reasonable period of time."

34 GOLF QUIZ

A. Remember how Gary Player took out his watch when his approach to the 17th hole in the 1974 British Open could not be found in the greenside rough, and began to clock his search?

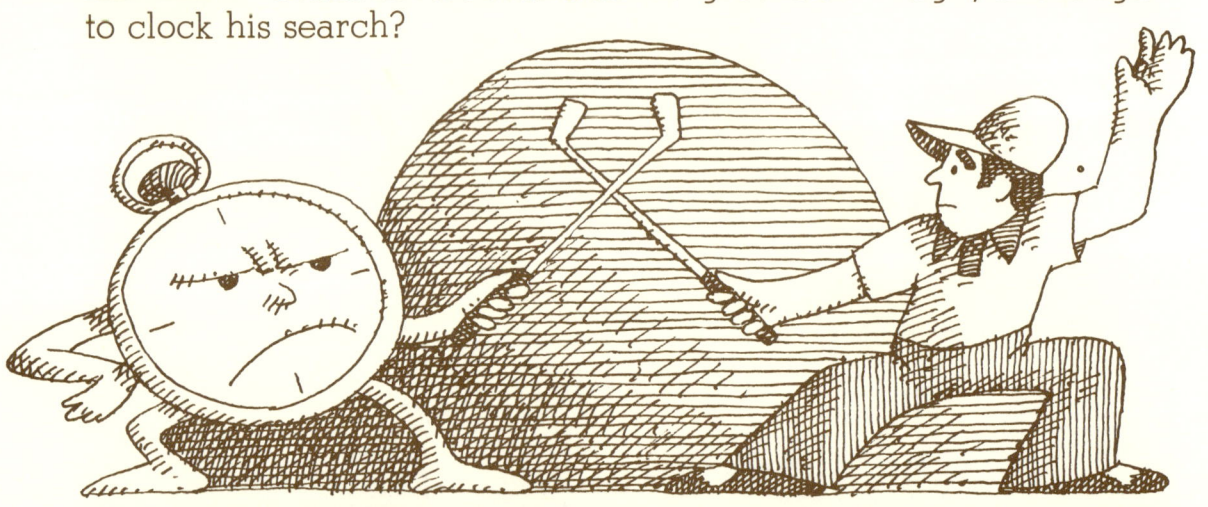

14

Only one of these statements is correct:

A. Although Henry Cotton described Mickey Wright as "the finest pupil I have been privileged to teach," Mickey was never at her best on British seaside courses.

B. Gene Sarazen was the first player to win the "Big Four": the Masters, the U.S. Open, the British Open, and our PGA Championship.

C. Two players who have gained tremendous added distance by using graphite shafts are Lee Trevino and Bill Casper.

D. If Walter Hagen had been a sound putter, there is no knowing how many titles he might have won.

36 GOLF QUIZ

B. Mickey was taught by Harry Pressler, primarily. Casper and Trevino haven't taken to graphite. There have been few finer putters than Hagen.

15

Only one of these statements about well-known women golfers is not true.

A. Hollis Stacy actually won the U.S. Girls' Junior Championship three years in a row—1969, 1970 and 1971.

B. Glenna Collett Vare won the U.S. Women's Amateur Championship six times in all—in 1922, 1925, 1928, 1929, 1930 and 1935. No one else has won one of our national championships six times.

C. The day after she won the 1954 U.S. Women's Open Championship with scores of 72, 71, 73 and 75, the phenomenal Babe Zaharias, playing left-handed, shot the championship course in 86.

D. Judy Rankin became the first woman golfer to earn over $100,000 in prize money in one season.

38 GOLF QUIZ

C. No, the day after the championship the Babe just took things easy.

GOLF QUIZ 39

16

Let us say you are a pro competing in a tournament administered by the PGA. In the course of a round, your ball finishes in a lie near a bridge railing that you feel is an artificial obstruction. You ask an official on the course whether or not you are entitled to relief without penalty. Invariably, he will take one of the four actions listed below:

A. You will be summarily informed that as a professional you are expected to know all the pertinent rules yourself. If you make the wrong decision, the penalty is assessed at the end of the round.

B. He will consult the current rules book and forthwith issue a ruling.

C. If the official is not sure of what the right ruling should be in your case, he will summon Jack Tuthill, the tournament director, via walkie-talkie. Tuthill will arrive post-haste by golf car, study the situation, and then make a ruling.

D. The new PGA rules computer will be called into service. If the appropriate buttons describing the situation are punched, a card containing the correct decision will immediately be spewed forth by the computer.

40 GOLF QUIZ

C. Tuthill is ubiquitous and tireless.

17 Nothing is ever unanimous, but most of the top golfers would have you believe that the best bunker player in the game today is

A. Jack Nicklaus.
B. Johnny Miller.
C. Gary Player.
D. Julius Boros.

42 GOLF QUIZ

c. Boros isn't too bad, though.

18 The man who carried the day in the first official U.S. Amateur was

A. Mark McCormack.
B. Keith MacKenzie.
C. Charles B. Macdonald.
D. Alister MacKenzie.

44 GOLF QUIZ

C. (Mark McCormack is the manager of Palmer and Player, among many other things. Keith MacKenzie is the secretary of the R.&A. Alister MacKenzie was a famous Scottish golf architect whose triumphs include the Augusta National, Cypress Point, and Royal Melbourne.)

19 In this day and age when golfers blithely hop around the world—this week Ballybunion, next week Bali Hai—one of the most remarkable members of this peripatetic tournament set includes among his titles the 1971 India Open, the 1972 Swiss Open, the 1973 Thailand Open, the 1974 Malaysian Open, the 1977 Sea Pines Heritage Classic and the 1979 Dutch Open. He is

- **A.** Dale Hayes of South Africa.
- **B.** Brian Barnes of England.
- **C.** Graham Marsh of Australia.
- **D.** Bob Byman of the United States.
- **E.** Bobby Cole of South Africa.

46 GOLF QUIZ

C. Marsh.

20

When Jim Dent won the long-driving contest at the first TPD Championship, the man who finished second with a poke of 312 yards was

A. John Schroeder.
B. Jumbo Ozaki.
C. Jack Nicklaus.
D. Tom Weiskopf.

48 GOLF QUIZ

Jim Dent

A. Dent's winning drive was about 12 yards longer.

21 In the 1975 Masters

A. Tom Weiskopf's putt on the 72nd green for a tie with Jack Nicklaus caught the corner of the cup but twisted out.

B. Gary Player, though out of the running, burned up the course in the last round with a record-tying 64.

C. Johnny Miller, after two disappointing rounds, got back in contention when he birdied six straight holes in the third round.

D. Lee Trevino, in one of his best showings ever at Augusta, had an outside chance to catch the leaders until he pulled his iron to the 11th into the water on the last day.

C. Miller birdied the second through the seventh. (Weiskopf's birdie putt on the 72nd did not hit the cup, just slid by it. Player did not have a 64 or any particularly hot round. Trevino was never really in the hunt.)

22

In the following list, there are four groups of four items. In only one instance, however, are all four items bona fide parts of the same overall category.

A. Lofter, track iron, cleek, driving niblick.
B. Dorothy Campbell Hurd, Joyce Wethered, Pam Barton, Catherine Lacoste.
C. Chandler Harper, Jock Hutchison, Tom Creavy, Ray Floyd.
D. Fescue, rye, red top, bourbon.

C. They were all winners of the PGA Championship. (The driving niblick was not a golf club. Joyce Wethered, unlike the other three foreign stars listed, never won the U.S. Women's Amateur. Bourbon is not a grass.)

23 Bob Hope used to refer to Jack Burke Jr. as

A. Jimmy Demaret's Secretary of Agriculture.
B. The pro from Boys' Town.
C. Doctor Rhythm.
D. The Man with the Golden Palm.

54 GOLF QUIZ

B. Jack was very young-looking for his age.

24

Listed below are groups of men golfers, golf holes, women golfers and golf implements all of whom or which have something in common. However, in one list there is one item that is definitely out of place. Which list is that?

A. Bob Murphy, Gene Littler, Jack Nicklaus, Freddy Haas, Ken Venturi.

B. The 12th at Augusta National, the 16th at Cypress Point, the fourth at Baltusrol (Lower Course), the 17th at Medinah, the 16th at Firestone.

C. Babe Didrikson, Wiffi Smith, Nancy Syms, Barbara McIntire, Carol Semple, Louise Suggs.

D. Blade, cash-in, flange-backed, bull's-eye, gooseneck, aluminum, mallet-head, Schenectady.

B. The 16th at Firestone is awry—it is a par-5 (with water) while the rest of the holes are par-3s (with water). The men golfers listed have all played on both the Walker Cup and Ryder Cup teams. The women golfers are Americans who have won the British Ladies' Championship. The fourth list is a variety of types of putters.

25

If, in 1925, someone came up to you and asked you if you would like a jigger, you would have been perfectly right to reply

A. Thank you, no. As long as we have Prohibition, I will obey the law of the land.

B. If you have an extra one, I'd love to have it. I really do like clubs with small, shallow faces, and I think I might get better results with a jigger than with either my mid-mashie or my mashie-iron.

C. It's very generous of you to offer me a handicap of two strokes out and two back, but I'd rather play you even, if you don't mind.

D. I would indeed. I'm tired of buying endless packages of wooden tees. I'd certainly like to try the new rubber tee from Australia that everyone's talking about.

58   GOLF QUIZ

B. Jiggers were also wonderful to chip with.

26

Here is a list of names of the wives of prominent golfers. Only one is wrong. Can you isolate it?

Edith Middlecoff
Louise Nelson
Barbara Nicklaus
Winnie Palmer
Shirley Player

Valerie Hogan
Shirley Casper
Jeanne Weiskopf
Vivien Jacklin
Shirley Littler

60   GOLF QUIZ

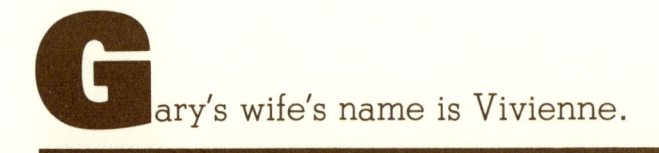

Gary's wife's name is Vivienne.

27

Everyone in golf is well acquainted with Ben Hogan's fabulous career but few people realize that

A. He is the only golfer who has swept the U.S. Open, the British Open, and the Masters in the same year.

B. He was 37 before he won his first U.S. Open.

C. His total of 276 at Riviera in 1948 was the record low score for the U.S. Open.

D. He won the British Open in 1953 by overtaking Bobby Locke and Peter Thomson on the last round with a spectacular 66, a record at Muirfield.

A. Hogan did this in his biggest year, 1953. He was 35 when he won his first U.S. Open in 1948. The U.S. Open record is 272. Finally, in the 1953 British Open, the men Hogan had to outplay in the final round were Roberto de Vicenzo—with whom he was tied after three rounds—and Dai Rees, Peter Thomson and Antonio Cerda—who he led by a stroke after three rounds. Ben's final round was a 68. The championship was held at Carnoustie, not Muirfield.

28

If a golf enthusiast referred to a hole as being quite similar to the famous 16th at Oakland Hills, he would be telling you about

A. A long par-3 over a huge pond to a terraced green.
B. A par-5 double-dogleg to a green entirely surrounded by sand.
C. A short par-5 doglegging to the left that can be reached in two if the player follows a big drive with a fine second over a creek guarding the green.
D. A medium-length par-4 to a cape-type green sticking boldly out into a pond.

64 GOLF QUIZ

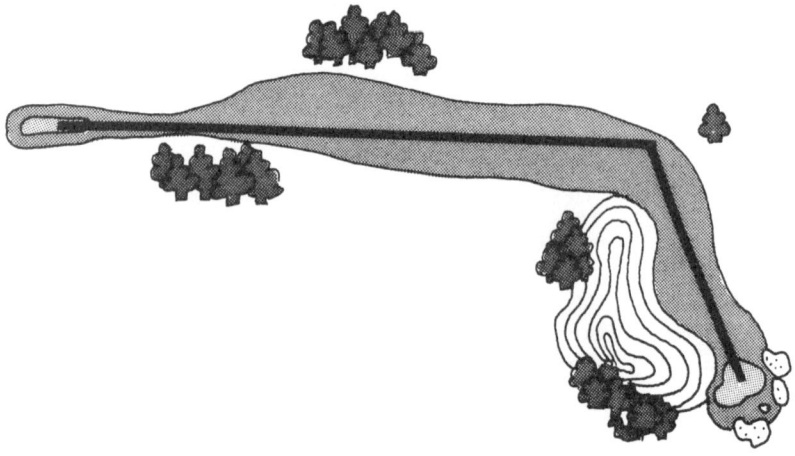

D. The hole is about 405 yards long, and the fairway is tight.

29 At the presentation ceremony following his epochal victory over Harry Vardon and Ted Ray at The Country Club in the 1913 U.S. Open, Francis Ouimet said:

A. "I simply tried my best to keep this cup from going to our friends across the water. I am very glad to have been the agency for keeping the cup in America."

B. "I am happy I brought this monster to its knees."

C. "Je ne parle pas anglais mais, entre nous, je cherche la plume de ma tante."

D. "I'm still in a daze. I always hoped to have the privilege of playing with Mr. Vardon and Mr. Ray, but I never dreamed that I could ever beat them."

A. A rather tricky one, admittedly. There is no reason why Ouimet might not have said (D). (A) is very grown-up language for a young man just turned 20, but Francis was an exceptional young man. But (C), nevaire, mon ami.

30

In 1876, the year of our nation's centennial celebration, the number of golf courses in the United States numbered exactly

- **A.** 22.
- **B.** 9.
- **C.** 0.
- **D.** 31.

68 GOLF QUIZ

C. The first permanent golf club in this country was not founded until 1888—St. Andrew's, in Yonkers.

31 There have been many dazzling finishes in tournament golf in recent years but only one man has ever won a major tournament by birdieing five of the last six holes. He is:

Jack Nicklaus   Tom Watson
Tommy Bolt   Lew Worsham
Art Wall   Leo Diegel
Gary Player   Johnny Miller

70 GOLF QUIZ

Art Wall, in the 1959 Masters. Nicklaus finished with five straight birdies in winning the Inverrary Classic in 1978, but that is not a major tournament.

32 Which one of these four statements is not true:

A. Ray Floyd often works out with his favorite baseball team, the Chicago Cubs.

B. When Gary Player is at his home outside Johannesburg, he devotes a large share of his time to his stable of race horses.

C. Hale Irwin, an outstanding football player at the University of Colorado, played one year of pro football with the Denver Broncos before deciding to turn to golf.

D. Charley Seaver, who was a member of our Walker Cup team in 1932, is the father of Tom Seaver, the great pitcher.

72 GOLF QUIZ

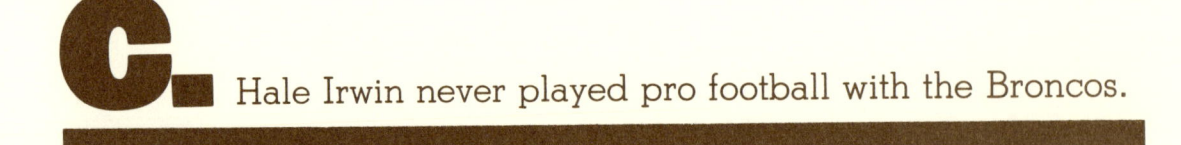

C. Hale Irwin never played pro football with the Broncos.

GOLF QUIZ 73

33
Donald Ross is credited with having a hand in the design of over 600 American courses. The list that follows, however, includes only one Ross course:

A. Pine Tree.
B. Pine Valley.
C. Pine Manor.
D. Pinehurst No. 2.

D. Pinehurst No. 2. Ross was affiliated with Pinehurst for most of his life. Dick Wilson built Pine Tree, and George Crump built Pine Valley. Pine Manor is a junior college for girls in Massachusetts.

34

Extract the one celebrity in the following list who is not a sponsor of a tour tournament:

Glen Campbell
Bob Hope
Andy Williams
Johnny Carson
Jackie Gleason
Danny Thomas
Sammy Davis

76 GOLF QUIZ

Johnny Carson. He's a tennis buff.

35

Tommy Armour was one of golf's greatest teachers—and one of its greatest characters as well. For many years he gave his lessons

A. In the plastic shelter he had specially fabricated so that he could continue to work with his pupils in the rainy weather so frequent in New Orleans.

B. On the old practice tee at Carnoustie, the course where he made his name by capturing the British Open.

C. On the superb practice ground that serves both the East Course and West Course at Winged Foot.

D. In Boca Raton, comfortably ensconced beside the practice tee in a canvas chair as he sipped a gin buck beneath a giant umbrella.

D. And in a very tall glass.

36

Jack Nicklaus has won a record 19 major championships. This magnificent achievement got under way when

A. He edged Gary Player in their playoff for the 1961 Masters when he birdied the 17th.

B. He nipped Julius Boros by a stroke in their stretch battle in the 1960 U.S. Open at Cherry Hills.

C. He outlasted Arnold Palmer in their playoff for the 1962 PGA title at Oakmont.

D. He defeated Charlie Coe with a birdie on the 36th green in the final of the 1959 U.S. Amateur.

80 GOLF QUIZ

D. Nicklaus holed for a birdie from eight feet on the 36th hole at Broadmoor. Coe's chip for his birdie from off the edge had stopped at the lip of the cup.

37

In 1975 Arnold Palmer, rousing himself from a protracted slump, carried off two tournaments. They were

- **A.** The Heritage Classic and the World Series of Golf.
- **B.** The Heritage Classic and the Byron Nelson Classic.
- **C.** The Byron Nelson Classic and the British PGA.
- **D.** The British PGA and the Spanish Open.

D. If Palmer had been British, he would have made their Ryder Cup team, for the points he piled up by his victories in the Spanish Open and the British PGA placed him high on the British Order of Merit.

38

When you prowl through the pages of the PGA Tour media guide, you find interesting personal items listed as part of the biographical sketches of touring stars past and present. For example, Ben Crenshaw goes in for bird-watching, Tom Kite for repairing golf clubs, Ed Sneed for backgammon and bridge. In the entry for Art Wall, one of the oldest golfers included, his listing under hobbies leaps out at you—it evokes so strongly his special personality. Can you select it?

- **A.** Collecting classic putters.
- **B.** Working around the house and yard.
- **C.** Collecting antique cars.
- **D.** Photographing sunrises and sunsets.

84 GOLF QUIZ

B. He has a particularly nice touch on the lawns.

39

At the last count, Robert Trent Jones, the peripatetic doyen of American golf course architects, had built courses in 32 countries. Listed below are the names of five Jones layouts and five islands, and the trick is to match them up correctly. You must get five out of five.

Pevero
Mauna Kea
Cotton Bay
Dorado Beach
Fountain Valley

St. Croix
Sardinia
Eleuthera (in the Bahamas)
Hawaii
Puerto Rico

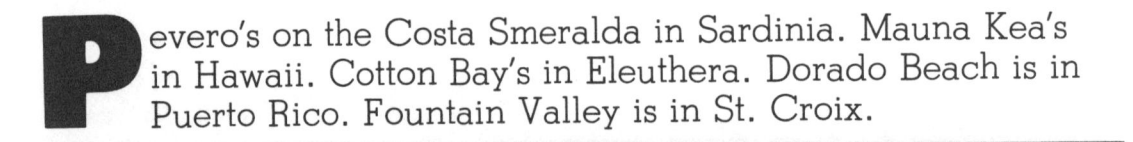

Pevero's on the Costa Smeralda in Sardinia. Mauna Kea's in Hawaii. Cotton Bay's in Eleuthera. Dorado Beach is in Puerto Rico. Fountain Valley is in St. Croix.

40 Select the correct statement.

A. The following courses are clustered on the Monterey peninsula: Cypress Point, Pebble Beach, Monterey Peninsula, Spyglass Hill.

B. The myriad courses in the Palm Springs-Palm Desert area include: Mission Hills, Dorado Beach, La Quinta, Indian Wells.

C. The following courses are located on the fine strip of linksland near the tip of Long Island: National Golf Links, Maidstone, Ekwanok, Shinnecock Hills.

D. The island of Bermuda can be properly proud of Mid-Ocean, Castle Harbour, Bermuda Dunes, Riddell's Bay.

88 GOLF QUIZ

A. Dorado Beach is in Puerto Rico, Ekwanok is in Vermont, and Bermuda Dunes is in the Palm Desert area.

GOLF QUIZ 89

41

When Tony Jacklin, the winner of the 1970 U.S. Open, opened his locker before the last round, he found that his good friends Bert Yancey and Tom Weiskopf had pasted the following injunction inside the locker:

- **A.** Keep The Ball in Play
- **B.** Tempo
- **C.** Walk With Old Man Par
- **D.** Cheers, Old Chap, You Can't Miss

90   GOLF QUIZ

B. Tempo.

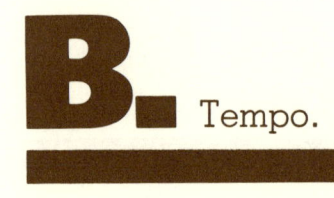

42

Everyone knows that Gene Sarazen made his historic double eagle in the 1935 Masters by holing a 4-wood for a 2 on the par-5 69th hole, but can you name the kind of shot Lew Worsham holed on the 72nd to edge Chandler Harper by one stroke in the 1953 edition of George S. May's rich World Championship?

A. He knocked a wedge shot of about 110 yards into the cup for a deuce on a shortish par-4.

B. He holed an "impossible" sand shot from a buried lie for a winning birdie.

C. On Tam O'Shanter's last hole, that difficult 177-yard par-3, Lew holed his tee shot, a beautifully struck 4-iron.

D. He semi-topped his 6-iron approach on the shortish par-4 but the ball struck the flagstick and dropped straight down into the cup.

A. Lew could always play the wedge.

43 This question deals with championship playoffs. All of the following statements are correct except one. Can you spot it?

A. The longest playoff in U.S. Open history occurred in 1931 when Billy Burke and George Von Elm battled over an extra 72 holes after tying in the championship proper. Burke won by a stroke.

B. The playoff between Bill Casper and Gene Littler for the 1970 Masters title was quite exceptional inasmuch as both men grew up in the San Diego area.

C. The last scheduled 36-hole playoff in a major championship took place in 1963 in the British Open. Bob Charles defeated Phil Rodgers in that double round.

D. One of the finest victories in Jack Nicklaus' career was scored in 1971 at Merion when he withstood a gallant last-ditch rally by Lee Trevino in their playoff for the U.S. Open and beat him by two strokes.

D. is incorrect. Trevino won the playoff with a 68 to Nicklaus' 71.

44

During the glory years of Bobby Jones' career, his exploits were reported, superbly, by a writer assigned by the Atlanta Journal. Jones' Boswell was

A. Henry McLemore
B. O. B. Keeler
C. Dudley (Waxo) Green
D. Grantland Rice

B. Keeler—Oscar Bane Keeler, with whom Jones collaborated on one of golf's great books, *Down The Fairway*.

45

If a golfer described a course as being quite similar to the renowned Pinehurst No. 2, no doubt he would have one of the following in mind:

A. An excellent Donald Ross course in which one of the features is the beautifully contoured undulations in the green area.

B. A typical A. W. Tillinghast course filled with pear-shaped greens set off by extremely deep bunkers.

C. One of those satanic Edmund Miller courses with at least seven water holes, many of them dogleg holes demanding long carries off the tee.

D. A tight, punitive Walter Travis design with some of the best features of Pinehurst's cousins, Shinnecock Hills and Merion.

A. Pinehurst No. 2 may be the finest chipping course in the world.

46

Listed below are two columns of names. The ones on the left are famous champions. The ones on the right are famous caddies, each of whom made his reputation caddieing for one of the champions. The idea is to match each of the players with the correct caddie.

Arnold Palmer   Eddie Lowery
Gene Sarazen   Angelo Argea
Jack Nicklaus   Creamy Carolan
Francis Ouimet   Stovepipe
Gary Player   Rabbit Dyer

GOLF QUIZ

The correct pairs are Palmer and Carolan, Sarazen and Stovepipe, Nicklaus and Argea, Ouimet and Lowery, Player and Dyer.

47

If you hit too long a drive off the first tee on the Old Course at St. Andrews, it may end up in

A. the Swilken Burn.
B. St. Andrews Bay.
C. The Eden River.
D. The pool at the Old Course Hotel.

102 GOLF QUIZ

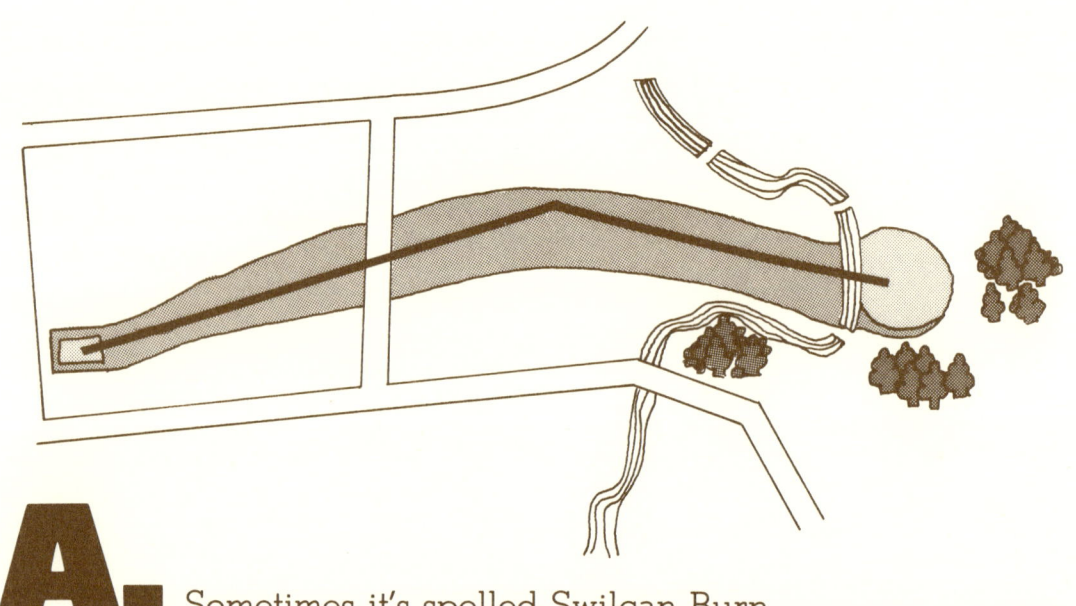

A. Sometimes it's spelled Swilcan Burn.

48

Ben Hogan was never one to go in for the ornate or pretentious. Accordingly, it was characteristic of Ben to name his new 36-hole golf club

A. The Golf Club
B. Hogan's Alley
C. The Country Club of Texas
D. The Trophy Club

D. The Trophy Club opened for play in 1977, but Hogan is no longer associated.

49

In the 1975 Walker Cup match at St. Andrews, Bill Campbell, warming up on the small practice green alongside the first hole, looked up and saw that his partner in his foursome match, John Grace, had only moments before driven off the first tee. Campbell therefore

A. Hurried to the first tee to play his drive, anxious that he should cause no delay in play.

B. Hurried to the official refereeing the match and reported that he had broken the rules by playing a practice stroke after his partner had teed off. The Americans were penalized loss of hole.

C. Hurried to the first tee, reported that he had discovered on the practice green that he had 15 clubs in his bag, and requested a ruling. No penalty was assessed since Campbell had not actually carried his bag onto the course until he had removed a club.

D. Hurried onto the course to congratulate Grace on a perfect drive that finished two yards short of the Swilken Burn. The American pair went on to win that hole when Campbell holed a touchy 11-footer.

106　GOLF QUIZ

B. Incidentally, the Americans lost that foursome 5 and 3.

50

Three of the four clusters below are made up of five items that have the same common denominator. Can you sift out the cluster in which one of the five items is inappropriate?

A. Pete Dye, Robert Von Hagge, Joe Lee, Robert McKenzie Jones, George Fazio
B. Azalea, Fire Thorn, Camellia, Holly, Red Bud
C. Killarney, Ballybunion, Portmarnock, Lahinch, Waterville
D. Principal's Nose, Road, Hell, Walkinshaw's, Cockle

108 GOLF QUIZ

A. It should be Robert Trent Jones in that cluster of golf course architects. B is made up of the names of holes at Augusta National, C of Irish courses, D of the names of bunkers at St. Andrews.

51

In Walter Hagen's day, British golf clubs did not permit professional golfers to change in the locker room. Hagen, with his usual aplomb, calmly solved this problem by

A. Changing at the local railroad station. That is why to this day the gents' room at British stations is referred to as "the Hagen."

B. Using the pro shop as his locker room. British club pros were only too happy to afford their colleague this small convenience.

C. Arriving at the course attired in white tie, top hat and tails. This was Walter's way of showing that he felt professional golfers should not be treated as laborers and were as good as anyone. He generally changed into his golf togs at a friend's house.

D. Hiring a Rolls Royce and, after being chauffered to the course, changing into his golf togs in the limousine.

110 GOLF QUIZ

D. Walter changed in the Rolls.

52 Who is the author of this classic humorous passage? "The least thing upset him on the links. He missed short putts because of the uproar of the butterflies in the adjoining meadows."

A. Bernard Darwin. It appears in his autobiography *The World That Fred Made.*

B. P. G. Wodehouse. It appears in his short story *Ordeal By Golf.*

C. Mark Twain. It appears in his great travel book *Innocents Abroad.*

D. Ring Lardner. It appears in his short story *Mr. Frisbie Sees It Through.*

112 GOLF QUIZ

B. Wodehouse.

53

When a golfer refers to Hell's Half Acre, he is obviously talking about

A. The enormous double green on the Old Course at St. Andrews which serves both the fifth and 13th holes.

B. The vast stretch of sand, sprinkled with bushes and other impedimenta, that runs the width of what normally would be fairway on the long seventh at Pine Valley.

C. The dramatic corner of the Augusta National where Rae's Creek curls alongside the greens on the 11th and 12th holes. The Masters has often been won and lost here.

D. The fantastic clubhouse at The Country Club, in Brookline, which has been the scene of so many wild parties.

114 GOLF QUIZ

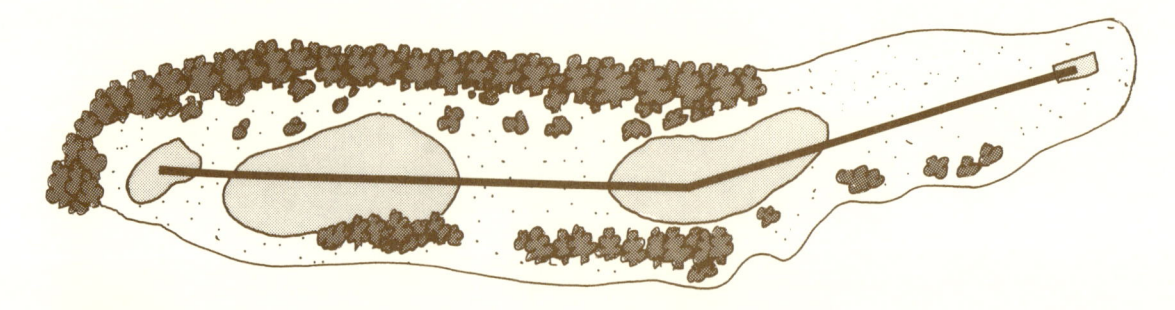

B. And you have to carry it with your second shot on this par-5 hole.

54 In the exciting stretch duel in the 1976 U.S. Open between Jerry Pate and John Mahaffey, Pate at length surged into the lead when he

A. Rolled in a six-footer for a birdie on the 215-yard 15th.
B. Sank a seven-footer for his par-4 on the 410-yard 16th, after which Mahaffey missed the five-footer he had for his par.
C. Got down in two putts from 45 feet on the 205-yard 17th, where Mahaffey took three putts from 50 feet.
D. Hit a magnificent 5-iron approach three feet from the pin on the 460-yard 18th after Mahaffey had put his second into the pond before the green.

116 GOLF QUIZ

C. That birdie on the last hole merely consolidated Pate's marvelous victory.

55 Once Arnold Palmer was well launched on his fabulous career, he was connected with many ancillary enterprises, among them a chain of laundries. This gave rise to the celebrated wisecrack, "The only pro I'd send my laundry to is Chen Ching-po." The author of this remark was

A. Dave Marr
B. Bob Drum
C. Lu Liang-huan
D. Mark McCormack

118　GOLF QUIZ

A. Marr.

56 One of the most famous replies in golf history was uttered by Joyce Wethered after she had holed a good-sized putt in the British Ladies' Championship at Troon despite the fact that a train had loudly clattered past the 11th green just as she was putting. Later, when she was asked if the train had disturbed her, Miss Wethered replied,

A. "It jolly well did. But one quickly gets used to trains if you play golf in this country."
B. "Yes, I should have waited."
C. "What train?"
D. "Yes, indeed. I probably would have written an angry letter to the Times had I missed the putt."

120 GOLF QUIZ

c. It dramatized her tremendous gift for concentration.

57 Read the following paragraph closely. Then answer true, it is a rule of golf, or false, it is just an exercise in dimpled prose.

"If a ball rests against the flagstick when it is in the hole, the player shall be entitled to have the flagstick removed, and if the ball falls into the hole the player shall be deemed to have holed out his last stroke; otherwise, the ball shall be placed on the lip of the cup, without penalty."

122 GOLF QUIZ

True. It is part of Rule 34-4.

58

We all know that Jack Nicklaus has won a record 19 major championships, but even the most scholarly Nicklausians are apt to forget that

A. He was extremely lucky to win the 1970 British Open. In his playoff with Doug Sanders, Sanders missed a three-footer on the home green that would have tied him with Nicklaus and forced a second playoff.

B. Included among those victories are two in the U.S. Amateur, registered in 1959 and 1961.

C. The hardest championship for Jack to win was our PGA. It eluded him until 1970 when he at last took that event at Southern Hills with one of his most unstoppable displays of shotmaking.

D. In that momentous playoff with his old rival, Arnold Palmer, in the 1962 U.S. Open, he finally pulled out in front by holing a twisting 40-foot putt for a birdie on the 16th.

B. In 1959 he defeated Charlie Coe 1 up in the finals, in 1961 he defeated Dudley Wysong 8 and 6.

59 This man's eventual triumphs in the "big ones" were eloquent testimony to his personal courage and stick-to-itiveness. In 1933 he lost the British Open in a playoff. In 1934 he lost in the final of our PGA Championship on the 38th hole. In 1935 he lost the Masters in a playoff. In 1939 he lost the U.S. Open in a playoff. Then in 1941 this very worthy golfer and gentleman had a change of luck: he won both the Masters and the U.S. Open. His name is

A. Lloyd Mangrum
B. Denny Shute
C. Craig Wood
D. Paul Runyan

126 GOLF QUIZ

C. Craig Wood.

60 Peter Thomson of Australia and Bobby Locke of South Africa dominated the British Open in the period following World War II. Between them, how many British Opens did these formidable invaders carry off?

A. 12
B. 7
C. 6
D. 9

D. Locke won the British Open in 1949-50-52-57, Thomson in 1954-55-56-58-65.

61 At the present time a good many of the outstanding amateur players are college undergraduates on golf scholarships, but there have always been career amateurs, well past college age, who have had to work for a living. For example, Billy Joe Patton is in the lumber business, Bill Campbell in the insurance business and Charlie Coe in the oil business. How did Bobby Jones make his living?

   A. He was a stockbroker.
   B. He worked in his father's export-import textile business.
   C. He was a lawyer.
   D. Having inherited a great deal of money, he was fortunate enough not to have to work and could devote all of his time to tournament golf.

130 GOLF QUIZ

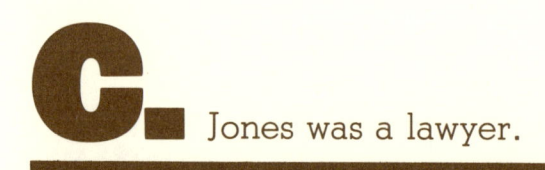

C. Jones was a lawyer.

62 When Bruce Lietzke surged to the fore in the winter of 1977, he created a considerable stir because

A. He hit the ball so hard that both feet were momentarily off the ground at impact.

B. He was the first American in years to deliberately play the pitch-and-run approach on our own courses whenever the green site encouraged it.

C. He employed the cross-handed method of putting—the left hand lower down the shaft than the right—and enjoyed marked success with it.

D. He occasionally liked to pick the ball clean off the sand in a bunker instead of always playing an explosion shot.

132 GOLF QUIZ

C. Lietzke putts cross-handed—and very effectively.

63 In the last few years a group of talented and colorful young Spanish golfers has performed sensationally in European tournaments. In the list that follows, only one of the persons in the lineup is *not* a member of the Spanish Explosion. Can you isolate him?

Antonio Garrido
Severiano Ballesteros
Angel Gallardo
Manuel Pinero

José Higueras
Salvador Balbueno
Francisco Abreu
Manuel Ballesteros

134 GOLF QUIZ

José Higueras. He is a Davis Cup tennis player.

64 One of these statements is incorrect. Which one is it?

A. In their famous playoff in the 1913 U.S. Open, Francis Ouimet actually beat the best ball of Harry Vardon and Ted Ray.

B. Arnold Palmer won the 1962 British Open by six shots.

C. In 1934 and 1935 Lawson Little won 31 consecutive matches in the U.S. and British Amateur Championships.

D. Lottie Dod, who had earlier won the Ladies' Lawn Tennis Championship at Wimbledon five times, was such a phenomenal athlete that she later won the British Ladies' Golf Championship.

A. Francis would have finished 1-down to the Britishers' best-ball.

65

There is no provision in the official Rules of Golf for a par-6 hole. True or false?

138   GOLF QUIZ

False. In referring to yardages for guidance in arriving at an appropriate par for a golf hole, the Rules of Golf suggest that a hole measuring 576 yards or more deserves serious consideration for being rated a par 6.

66 Tom Kite and Ben Crenshaw both grew up at the same golf club and were taught by the same professional. Can you correctly name the club and the club professional?

A. The club was the Broadmoor in Colorado Springs and the professional was Dow Finsterwald.
B. The club was the Champions in Houston and the professional was Jack Burke Jr.
C. The club was the Country Club of Austin and the professional was Harvey Penick.
D. The club was the Gulf and Southern Golf Club in Dallas and the professional was Dave Marr.

140 GOLF QUIZ

C. They were taught by Harvey Penick at the C.C. of Austin.

67

Three of the four groups listed below are made up, you might say, of items that belong to the same species—that share something in common. One group, however, doesn't fit this description: one of its items is definitely out of place. Which group is it?

A. Onwentsia, Glen View, Medinah, North Shore and Olympia Fields.

B. Mickey Wright, Judy Rankin, Amy Alcott, Hollis Stacy and Marlene Bauer.

C. Midiron, spade mashie, mashie iron, jigger and mashie niblick.

D. Lionel Hebert, Jock Hutchison, Vic Ghezzi, Walter Burkemo and Ray Floyd.

B. Wright, Alcott, Stacy and Bauer all won the USGA Girls' Junior Championship, but Rankin did not. The first group is comprised of courses in the Chicago area which have hosted the U.S. Open. The third group is made up of old-time golf clubs. The men in the fourth group all won the PGA Championship.

68

In 1977 he won the World Senior Professional Championship for the second time. For years he was known as "the best foul-weather golfer in the world." He is

- **A.** Stan Leonard of Canada.
- **B.** Roberto de Vicenzo of Argentina.
- **C.** Kel Nagle of Australia.
- **D.** Peter Alliss of England.
- **E.** Dai Rees of Wales.
- **F.** Bob Toski of the United States.
- **G.** Christy O'Connor of Ireland.

144 GOLF QUIZ

G. Christy's the boy.

69

Only one of the following statements about the 1960 U.S. Open at Cherry Hills, in Denver, is incorrect.

A. Jack Fleck was very much in the running until the last nine and finished in a tie for third.

B. On the final day, Ben Hogan, making his last real bid for the title, hit the first 34 greens in regulation.

C. Arnold Palmer's exciting victory was due to his fantastic finish in which he birdied six of the last seven holes.

D. Jack Nicklaus, a mere lad of 20, actually took over the lead in the championship with six holes left to play.

146 GOLF QUIZ

C. Arnie birdied six of the *first* seven holes enroute to a final round of 65 that won him the championship.

70 What distinguished politician made the following pronouncement about the virtues of golf: "A tolerable day, a tolerable green, a tolerable opponent ought to supply all that any reasonably constituted human being should require in the way of entertainment. The golfer should find no difficulty in dismissing all worries from his mind and regarding golf, even if it be indifferent golf, as the true and adequate end of man's existence. Care may sit behind the horseman, she never presumes to walk with the caddie."

- **A.** Theodore Roosevelt, the American President.
- **B.** Winston Churchill, the British prime minister.
- **C.** Jack Westland, the American Congressman.
- **D.** Prince Konoye, the Japanese foreign minister.
- **E.** Arthur Balfour, the British prime minister.
- **F.** James Michael Curley, the mayor of Boston.
- **G.** Cato the Elder, the Roman senator.

148 GOLF QUIZ

E. The Rt. Hon. A. J. Balfour.

71

Quite a few people have combined golf and tennis successfully. Indeed, three of the following four statements are correct. Which one is not?

A. Lottie Dod, who won five women's singles championships at Wimbledon between 1887 and 1893, gradually drifted into golf, and in 1904 won the British Ladies' Golf Championship.

B. Catherine Lacoste de Prado, who has won the U.S. Women's Amateur and Open titles, as well as the British Ladies', is the daughter of René Lacoste who won two United States and two Wimbledon singles championships and later added the 1934 French Amateur golf championship.

C. Ellsworth Vines, the victor at Forest Hills in 1931 and 1932 and at Wimbledon in 1932, became a professional golfer after closing out his career in tennis.

D. In 1924 Mary K. Browne not only reached the semifinals of our national women's tennis championship—she really extended Helen Wills before going down 6-4, 4-6, 6-3—but two weeks later she reached the finals of our national women's golf championship by beating Glenna Collett on the 19th hole in their semifinal match.

150 GOLF QUIZ

B. Rene Lacoste was an accomplished golfer but he never won the French Amateur. However, Catherine's mother, Simone Thion de la Chaume, won the British Ladies' Golf Championship in 1927.

72

The late Bing Crosby not only had a thoroughgoing love of golf but played the game extremely well. Indeed, only one of these statements is not true.

A. He first developed his smooth, rhythmic swing as a caddie at the Spokane Country Club.

B. During his days as a member of the Lakeside Club in North Hollywood, he was club champion five times and played to a 2-handicap.

C. He was one of the few golfers who scored a hole-in-one on the famous 16th at Cypress Point, the par 3 over the Pacific to the cliff-edged green.

D. In 1950, when he played in the British Amateur, he won his first two matches.

152 GOLF QUIZ

D. Bing lost his first-round match in the British Amateur, but he played a most respectable round. He started by birdieing two of the first three holes.

73

Tom Watson made it clear that he owed an incalculable debt to one man when he achieved his dramatic victory over Jack Nicklaus in the 1977 Masters. Who was that man and what did he do for Tom?

A. Byron Nelson, his golf tutor. Byron told him to slow down the tempo of his swing, the pace of his walk, the speed of his waggle—everything.

B. Miller Barber, the veteran touring pro. Miller spotted a loop in Watson's backswing and helped him to get back on the orthodox track.

C. Dr. Gil Morgan. Morgan, a doctor of optometry, examined Watson's eyes on the eve of the tournament and rid him of the haunting worry that his lack of depth perception was due to astigmatism.

D. Gerald Micklem. Micklem, the lovable old Stanford golf coach who helped develop Watson's game, phoned him after the first round and told him that he was standing too close to the ball after hitting it.

A. Nelson has worked to slow down the fast tempo at which Watson does most things.

74 True or false: The golf ball we play today in the United States—the so-called "big ball" which is 1.68 inches in diameter and 1.62 ounces in weight—was adopted in 1932.

156 GOLF QUIZ

True. The year was 1932.

75 One of Sam Snead's most hilarious imitations is of an old foe of his who was not a great stylist but who could get the ball in the cup in a small number of strokes because he was such an incredible putter. In his imitation, Snead puffs out his cheeks, assumes a closed putting stance, performs a long and sweeping putting stroke, and then, almost as soon as he has dispatched the ball on its way to the hole, tips the brim of an imaginary cap to acknowledge that he has holed the putt or that he will have holed it just as soon as the ball reaches the cup. The subject of Sam's imitation is

A. Lloyd Mangrum.
B. Bobby Locke.
C. Horton Smith.
D. Harry Bradshaw.

158 GOLF QUIZ

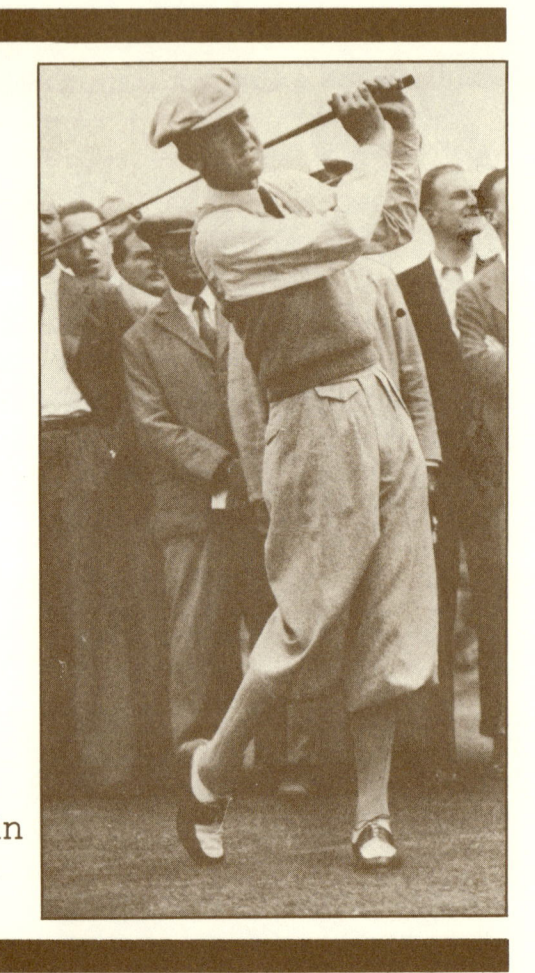

B. Bobby Locke, old "Muffin Face," always wore that rumpled white cap.

76

Only one of these statements is incorrect:

A. Debbie Austin, who suddenly bloomed as a multiple winner on the LPGA Tour, has been laboring in the vineyard as a pro since 1968.

B. There is no question that the finest clinic given by a golfer, male or female, is the one that Patty Berg has conducted for years.

C. Jo Ann Prentice used her earnings from the tour to invest in a successful chain of sportswear stores in her native Texas.

D. Laura Baugh has yet to win a professional tournament, but she has made plenty of yen in Japan where calendars featuring her are best-sellers.

160   GOLF QUIZ

c. Jo Ann owns a golf club in her native Alabama.

77 It is one of the most famous finishing holes in golf. It is so short it can be driven. But it also can be very difficult, mainly because of the large, low basin that occupies the front left part of the green and is called the Valley of Sin. This hole is the

- **A.** 18th at Muirfield
- **B.** 18th at Royal Hong Kong
- **C.** 18th at the Old Course, St. Andrews
- **D.** 18th at the New Course, St. Andrews

162 GOLF QUIZ

D. Overlooking the green is the headquarters of the Royal & Ancient Golf Club.

78

Only one of these statements is true. Which one is it?

A. Only one foreign golfer has won the U.S. Amateur Championship since Ross Somerville did it in 1932.

B. No golfer has ever made seven consecutive birdies in a PGA Tour event.

C. No golfer has ever won the PGA Championship four years in a row.

D. People have done some pretty fancy scoring in the Masters, but nobody has ever played the last two rounds in 10 strokes under par.

164 GOLF QUIZ

A. The only foreign winner of the U.S. Amateur since 1932 has been Gary Cowan, of Canada, who captured it twice, in 1966 and 1971. Bob Goalby put together eight straight birdies in 1961, and Fuzzy Zoeller tied that record in 1976. Walter Hagen won the PGA Championship in four successive years, 1924 through 1927. In the memorable 1975 Masters, Johnny Miller played the last two rounds in 65 and 66, a full 13 strokes under par.

79

Graham Marsh, the pleasant Australian who enjoyed his first successful U.S. tour campaign in 1977, turned to golf after starting out as

- **A.** A stand-out cricketer.
- **B.** A teacher of mathematics.
- **C.** A wool salesman.
- **D.** A Qantas pilot.

166 GOLF QUIZ

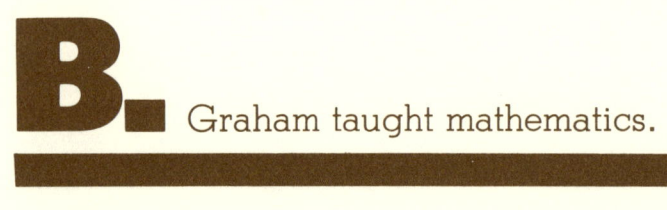

B. Graham taught mathematics.

80 Take the number of major championships Jack Nicklaus has won; subtract three; divide this by the number of putts Hubert Green took on the 72nd green of the 1977 U.S. Open; multiply this by the number of times the British team has won the Walker Cup; multiply this by the number of persons from whom a tournament golfer is permitted in stroke-play singles competition to ask information about the club he should use on his upcoming shot; subtract the number of 18-hole golf courses in Russia at the present time. What answer do you arrive at?

    A.   3
    B. 16
    C.   6
    D. 10
    E. 12

168 GOLF QUIZ

B. 16. It is arrived at this way. Take the number of Nicklaus' victories, 19; subtract three; divide it by 2 (the number of Green's putts on the 72nd). That gives you 8. Eight times two (the number of British victories in the Walker Cup series) is 16. Sixteen times one—the golfer's caddie is the only person he can ask for information of this nature—is 16. Sixteen minus zero—there are no golf courses in Russia—gives you a final answer of 16.

81 Andrew Kirkaldy, the early Scottish professional, was a "rough pebble" who was noted for his native wit. For example, once when he was asked, "Andrew, how is the world treating you?" he made the following memorable reply:

A. "Jus' a wee deoch and dorris."
B. "Hell, mon, I got the yips."
C. "Verra seldom."
D. "Mild and bitter, bitter and mild."

170　GOLF QUIZ

C. "Verra seldom."

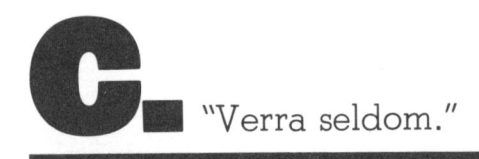

82

In three of the following four groups, each of the items named has something in common with the others. However, in one of the groups one of the items has no affinity whatsoever with its neighbors. Which group is that?

A. Chick Evans, Jerry Travers, Bobby Jones, Francis Ouimet, Jack Nicklaus.

B. Kittansett, Milwaukee Country Club, National Golf Links, Pine Valley, Five Farms.

C. Dick Siderowf, Charlie Yates, Frank Stranahan, Bob Dickson, Joe Conrad.

D. St. Andrews, Hoylake, Interlachen, Winged Foot, Merion.

D. Winged Foot is out of place—Bobby Jones compiled his Grand Slam in 1930 on the other four courses. It was the year before that he won our Open at Winged Foot. The golfers in A are all former U.S. Amateur champions. B is made up of courses on which the Walker Cup has been played in this country. The golfers in C are some Americans who have carried off the British Amateur.

83

If someone asked you the derivation of the word "caddie," you would be right on the mark if you answered that it comes from

A. The Scottish verb "cadle," which means to carry a bag of some size.

B. The French noun "cadet," which, in its several definitions, refers to a young man who holds a certain post.

C. The Welsh, the first caddie-master at Harlech being Owen Cadwallader.

D. American slang, being a home-bred invention like eagle, birdie, out-of-bounds and 19th hole.

174 GOLF QUIZ

B. Believe it or not, it comes from the French.

84

All of these statements about Nancy Lopez are correct except one. Which one is that?

A. She started hitting golf balls when she was 8, using a 4-wood her father had given her.

B. Like Jack Nicklaus, who never won the U.S. Junior championship, Nancy never succeeded in winning the U.S. Girls' Junior championship.

C. In 1977, before attending the LPGA qualifying school, and qualifying with distinction, she finished second in the U.S. Women's Open.

D. In 1978 she broke all LPGA records by winning five tournaments in five consecutive starts.

176　GOLF QUIZ

B. Nancy won the Girls' Junior twice.

85

Match up these five fine golfers with the university they attended. You must align them all correctly.

Ben Crenshaw   Brigham Young
Hale Irwin   Stanford
Tom Weiskopf   Texas
Tom Watson   Ohio State
Johnny Miller   Colorado

178   GOLF QUIZ

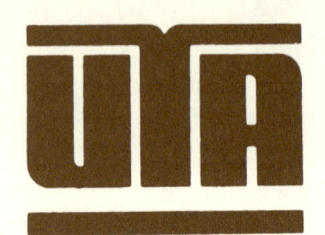

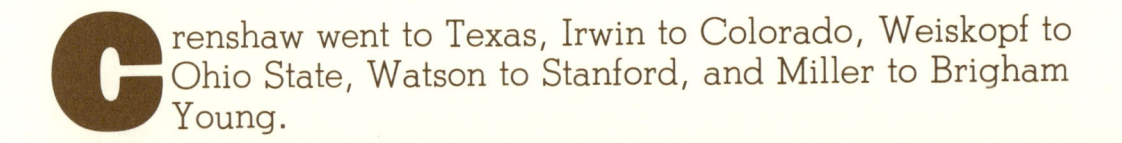

Brigham Young University

The Ohio State University

Crenshaw went to Texas, Irwin to Colorado, Weiskopf to Ohio State, Watson to Stanford, and Miller to Brigham Young.

86

Name the golfer from whose autobiography the following passage is taken, and name the tournament (the year as well as the event) that he is describing.

"We were followed by a sparse gallery, for the bulk of the spectators were watching Jones or Wood and Picard, who were playing three holes ahead of us. It was about 5:30 in the afternoon when Walter and I came to the 15th hole. . ."

180 GOLF QUIZ

Gene Sarazen. In this excerpt he is, of course, beginning the description of his historic double-eagle in the 1935 Masters.

87

This is a two-part question. You must answer both parts correctly.

A. What rising young professional has won tournaments in England, France, Switzerland, Japan, United States, the Philippines, Kenya, New Zealand and Germany?

B. What was his first tournament victory on the American tour?

182 GOLF QUIZ

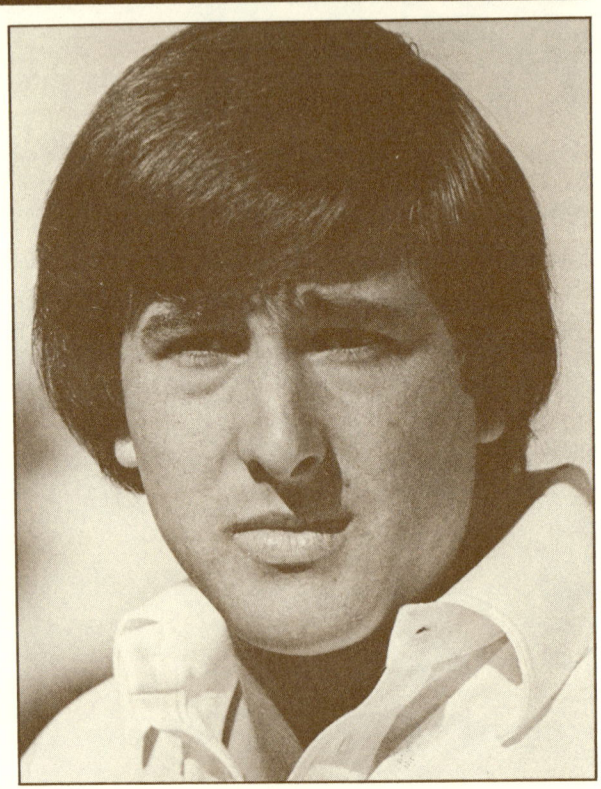

Severiano Ballesteros. In 1978 he won the Greater Greensboro Open.

88 The first golf club established outside of Scotland and England was:

A. Royal Hong Kong, which dates from 1853 when Queen Victoria's emissary, Lord Salisbury, drove off the first ball.

B. Royal Calcutta. Its early members included a high proportion of Scots from the Dundee area who were in the jute trade in Bengal and were homesick for their national game.

C. Royal Montreal, which was carved out of the wilderness in 1873 by Gerald François Micklem, the French-Canadian fur trapper who turned golf course architect in middle age and built such famous courses as Banff and Labrador Springs.

D. Van Cortlandt Park. Constructed by the early Dutch settlers in the upper reaches of New York City, this course retained some of the characteristics of the Dutch game of kolven, but historians believe that it was, and is, essentially a bonafide golf links.

184 GOLF QUIZ

B. Royal Calcutta.

89

Harvey Penick, the well-known professional long associated with the Austin (Tex.) Country Club, has taught many fine players, both men and women, who have enjoyed considerable success on the pro tours. From the following list, cull the two protégés of Penick's who in recent years have done very well indeed on the PGA Tour:

Ben Crenshaw
Jim Simons
Charles Coody
Jerry Pate

John Mahaffey
Tom Kite
Hubert Green
Mark Hayes

186 GOLF QUIZ

Crenshaw and Kite. Both their families are members of the club.

90

Billy Burke won the 1931 U.S. Open at Inverness, in Ohio, after an historic playoff with George Von Elm. Their playoff lasted:

A. Just two holes, Burke winning the first sudden-death playoff ever with a birdie on the second.
B. 36 holes.
C. 18 holes.
D. 72 holes.

D. They finished in a tie in a 36-hole playoff, so a second 36 holes was decreed. Burke won by a single stroke.

91

This golfer won a national championship at Baltusrol by playing the last 36 holes in 69-72—141, three under par.

A. Mickey Wright.
B. Bobby Jones.
C. Tony Manero.
D. Babe Didrikson.

190 GOLF QUIZ

A. Mickey did this in the 1961 U.S. Open. Many consider it the best day's golf ever played by a woman.

92

In 1954, all of these things, except one, happened. Can you isolate it?

A. An unknown young amateur, Billy Joe Patton, fought it out all the way in the Masters with Snead and Hogan, only to lose by a single stroke.

B. The U.S. Open was telecast nationally for the first time.

C. Arnold Palmer won his first major title, the U.S. Amateur, at the Country Club of Detroit.

D. Ben Hogan won a thrilling British Open at Muirfield with a total of 271.

E. Babe Zaharias, in a gallant performance, won her third and last U.S. Women's Open, edging out the runner-up by a mere 12 strokes.

D. Ben won the British Open the year before, at Carnoustie with a total of 282.

93

Gary Player, whose inventiveness and gift for hard work know no bounds, trotted out a new wrinkle in 1978 that served him well.

A. He gave all of his black sportshirts and black slacks to Goodwill Industries and began appearing in clothes that ran the gamut of the colors of the rainbow.

B. Deciding that accuracy is far more critical than distance off the tee, he jettisoned his driver and began using his 2-wood. His victory in the 1978 Masters depended first and foremost on his brilliant positioning of his tee shots.

C. After putting for decades with a short, jabby stroke, he successfully developed a smooth through-the-ball stroke.

D. Deciding that he needed to get into far better physical condition, he spent a full month at Jimmy Demaret's Shape-Up School in Houston before playing a shot on the American tour.

194   GOLF QUIZ

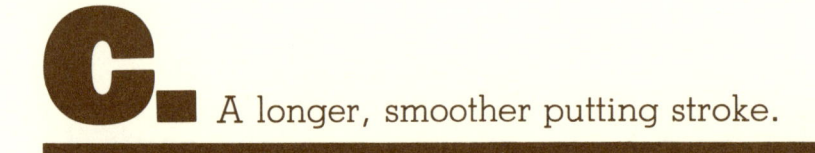

c. A longer, smoother putting stroke.

94

Five bridges on the Old Course at St. Andrews span the Swilken Burn. Two bridges at Oakmont span the Monongahela River. Several bridges at Carnoustie span the coiling Barry Burn. Two bridges at Augusta National span Rae's Creek. One of these statements doesn't hold water. Which one is it?

196 GOLF QUIZ

The bridge at Oakmont spans the Pennsylvania Turnpike.

95

Of the four statements that follow, how many are incorrect?

A. Sandy Tatum, past president of the USGA, was a star golfer at Stanford and also played at Oxford.

B. The American-sized golf ball is now mandatory in practically all the important British professional tournaments.

C. Simone Thion de la Chaume, who married René Lacoste, was the first French golfer to win the British Ladies' Championship. Her daughter Catherine also won that title.

D. The winner of the 1973 Masters was a Georgian—Tommy Aaron.

GOLF QUIZ

None. They're all correct statements.

96

Take one player from Column A and one description from column B and match them. You must come up with four correct matches.

Hsieh Min-nan   a solid golfer from Burma
Ben Arda   a fine player from Taiwan
Jumbo Ozaki   a veteran from the Philippines
Mye Aye   a long-hitting Japanese star

200   GOLF QUIZ

Hsieh is from Taiwan, Arda from the Philippines, Ozaki from Japan, and Aye from Burma.

97 When Sam Snead came out of the backwoods and was breaking into the pro tour in the mid-1930s, he won a big tournament on the West Coast. A day or so later he was shown a New York newspaper that carried a story of his victory along with a photograph of him. Taken aback, Sam said:

A. Why couldn't they have run a picture of me with my coconut straw on?

B. How'd they ever get a picture of me? I ain't ever been to New York.

C. That's typical. The picture's a year old and was taken on a practice tee in West Virginia.

D. It's a lousy shot of my swing, but after they send me the check for the picture, I probably won't be so critical.

202 GOLF QUIZ

B. "How'd they ever get a picture of me?..."

98 What unsung contemporary G. K. Chesterton made epigrammatical history when he said of Nicklaus: "He has become a legend in his spare time."

A. Chi Chi Rodriguez.
B. Norm Crosby.
C. Jim Murray.
D. Lee Trevino.

204 GOLF QUIZ

A. Chi Chi.

99

What taste in golf apparel did Bobby Locke, Ben Hogan, Bill Campbell, Ken Venturi, Gardner Dickinson and Bob Toski share?

206 GOLF QUIZ

They all prefer to wear a flat white cap with a straight, wide visor.

100 In winning the U.S. Open at Cherry Hills on the 72nd hole, a long and treacherous par 4 to a raised green, Andy North's third shot was:

A. A well-judged 45-foot approach putt that finished six inches from the cup and insured his victory.

B. A nice little chip from the front fringe of the green that left him a two-footer.

C. A poorly played explosion shot that bounced over the green and left him with the difficult job of getting down in two from the rough behind the green.

D. A poorly played little wedge shot from the rough on the left that didn't even reach the green and, instead, plopped into one of the front bunkers.

D. But after that very poor third, North saved the 5 he needed to win with a courageous sand shot about 3½ feet from the hole.

101

There was a time when it was more common than it is today to give holes not only a number but a distinctive name. One such hole that most followers of golf should know of is the par 3 that is called the "Postage Stamp" because of its very small green. It is

- **A.** The seventh hole at Hoylake.
- **B.** The 12th hole at Augusta National.
- **C.** The eighth hole at Troon.
- **D.** The seventh hole at Pebble Beach.

210 GOLF QUIZ

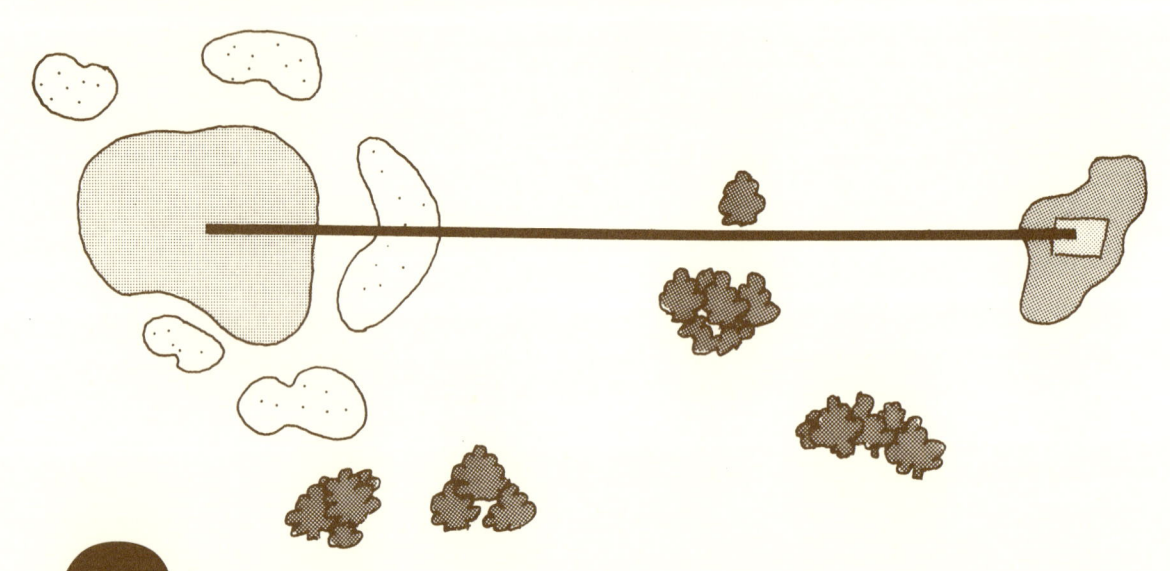

C. The eighth at Troon. Remember when Sarazen aced it in 1973?

102

All of the players listed below except one have earned more than a million dollars in prize money on our tournament circuit. Isolate the player who has not reached that figure.

Arnold Palmer
Jack Nicklaus
Ben Hogan
Bruce Crampton
Julius Boros

Miller Barber
Johnny Miller
Dave Hill
Raymond Floyd

Hogan, ironically. In his day the *total* prize money at most tournaments was only $10,000 or $15,000.

103

The first of the four major championships in which a sudden-death playoff was used to determine the winner was

A. The PGA Championship. In 1977 Lanny Wadkins and Gene Littler played off for the title at Pebble Beach.

B. The British Open. In 1963 Bob Charles and Phil Rodgers played off for the title at Lytham and St. Annes.

C. The U.S. Open. In 1975 Lou Graham and John Mahaffey played off for the title at Medinah.

D. The Masters. In 1979 Fuzzy Zoeller, Ed Sneed and Tom Watson played off for the title.

214 GOLF QUIZ

A. Wadkins defeated Littler on the third extra hole.

104 Over the last 60-odd years, the Pine Valley Golf Club, in Clementon, N.J., has been known as "the most difficult golf course in the world." More to the point, it is one of the finest tests of golf in the world. It was designed by

A. Donald Ross, the Scottish-born genius, who, incidentally, also designed Pinehurst No. 2, Pine Needles and Pine Tree.

B. Walter Travis, who had just finished his work on Garden City and was avid for new challenges. When his friend Chauncey Depew Steele showed him the wonderful plot of natural golf land in Clementon, Travis dropped all other plans.

C. Dr. Alister Mackenzie, who built it just after he had completed Cypress Point. Mackenzie regarded it as his chef d'oeuvre.

D. George Crump, a Philadelphia hotel owner, who virtually camped out at the heavily wooded property from 1912 until 1918 when the dream he was obsessed with became a reality.

D. George Crump. Another amateur architect, Hugh Wilson, supplied the finishing touches after Crump's death.

105

Only one answer is correct. The rubber-cored Haskell ball, which replaced the gutta percha ball,

A. Owed its first acceptance to the fact that it was a "floater"—if you hit it into a water hazard, you could spot it and retrieve it.

B. Made its first real popular impact when Walter Travis used it in winning the U.S. Amateur Championship in 1901.

C. Was invented by Raymond Haskell, an outstanding Scottish industrial chemist, who was a member of Muirfield.

D. Was banned by the PGA for several years, following its introduction in 1910, on the grounds that its length rendered many tour courses obsolete.

218   GOLF QUIZ

B. The PGA, by the way, was not formed until 1916.

106

Only one of the following statements is incorrect:

A. Enroute to winning the San Diego Open in 1955, Tommy Bolt racked up seven consecutive birdies. More than that, his approaches on those seven holes finished six, six, three, eight, four, four and four feet respectively from the pin.

B. That same winter—1955—Mike Souchak set a scoring record that has yet to be equaled on the PGA Tour. In his first round in the Texas Open, he shot the second nine in 27 strokes: birdie, par, par, eagle, birdie, birdie, birdie, birdie, birdie.

C. Johnny Miller's phenomenal closing round of 63, which won him the 1973 Open at redoubtable Oakmont, depended primarily on his finishing rush: four birdies on the last five holes.

D. Tom Watson stood two shots behind Jack Nicklaus, with whom he was paired, with six holes remaining in the 1977 British Open. He overtook and passed Nicklaus by playing those last six holes in birdie, par, birdie, par, birdie, birdie.

C. Miller wrought his havoc on the first 13 holes, racking up eight birdies.

107 Which wonderful golfer's career reached some of its highest points at Southern Hills in 1946, Gullane in 1947, Atlantic City Country Club in 1948, Rolling Hills Country Club in 1950 and Salem Country Club in 1954?

Babe Didrikson Zaharias. She won her five national championships at those sites—the U.S. Women's Amateur at Southern Hills, the British Ladies at Gullane and the U.S. Women's Open at Atlantic City, Rolling Hills and Salem.

108

Japan, as we know, is golf mad—maybe the most golf-mad country in the world. This national infatuation with the game began in:

A. 1858, when Commodore Perry, who "opened up" Japan, presented the emperor with three sets of clubs that had been specially made by Gerald Micklem, the famous English clubmaker.

B. 1921, when Mitsujiro Watanabe, a research chemist at Waseda University, invented the modern rubber-cored ball.

C. 1971, when Jumbo Ozaki, the former baseball star, defeated Sam Snead, Lee Trevino, Roberto de Vicenzo, and Tom Weiskopf in successive 36-hole television matches, all presented in prime time on the national network.

D. 1957, when the Japanese team of Pete Nakamura and Koichi Ono staggered the golf world by winning the Canada Cup.

D. And Nakamura also had the low individual score for the four rounds. (The U.S. team of Snead and Demaret just did not have it on the last day.)

109

Three of the four groups listed below are composed of people, places or things that share something in common. However, one of these groups fails to meet this description. Which one is it?

A. Mickey Wright, Donna Caponi Young, Susie Berning, Hollis Stacy, JoAnne Carner.
B. The Old Course, the New Course, the Fife Course, the Jubilee Course, the Eden Course.
C. Dynamiter, Sure Out, Sand Wedge, Blaster, Sand Iron.
D. Art Bell, Bob Toski, Harry Obitz, Jack Grout, Claude Harmon.

226 GOLF QUIZ

B. There's no Fife Course at St. Andrews. The golfers in the first group have each won the U.S. Women's Open twice or more. The clubs in the third group are various names given by manufacturers to their wedges. The fourth group is composed of well-known teaching professionals.

110 If any one single shot won the 1979 U.S. Open for Hale Irwin, it was

A. The great 2-iron he ripped three feet from the pin on the par-5 13th at Inverness on his third round.

B. The bunker shot he holed from the steep-walled front bunker on the 10th, which set up his second round of 67 and put him in front to stay.

C. The eight-footer he holed to save his par on the 17th on the final day when he had thrown away all but two strokes of his once commanding lead.

D. His tee shot on the 18th on the final round, which finished in the middle of the fairway and made it almost certain that he would get the par he needed.

228 GOLF QUIZ

A. Irwin's eagle on the 13th was the key thrust in a 67 that put him in the lead after the third round.

111 If you were caddieing for an old-time golfer and he asked you to let him have his baffy, you would have made the right move if you handed him

A. His sweater, a close-knit Shetland with a high collar, which was particularly popular with golfers because it was semi-waterproof.

B. A wooden club, the precursor of today's 3-wood and 4-wood, which had a nice, manageable head with a distinctly lofted face, and was the favorite fairway wood of many golfers.

C. A small flask filled with a liqueur called kümmel which nearly every high-strung golfer carried along since it was believed that a quick shot of it steadied the nerves.

D. The first really effective golf glove, made of wool with a leather palm, which kept the left hand warm and also strengthened its grip on the club.

B. You wouldn't have been wrong, though, to have reminded him about the kümmel and to have added how much you liked the flavor of caraway seeds yourself.

112

"Golf is a good walk spoiled." The author of this slur was

A. Winston Churchill, who turned down repeated invitations to join the Royal & Ancient Golf Club of St. Andrews.

B. Max Beerbohm, the famous head pro at the Baden-Baden Racquet & Tennis Club.

C. Mark Twain, who was not entranced by the cult of games or strenuous exercise in general.

D. Jay Gatsby, who was attempting to hide his chagrin on receiving the news that he had been blackballed by the Little Egg Golf Club.

232　GOLF QUIZ

c. Mark Twain.

113 You are bunkered close to a green. In preparing to play your recovery, you make sure not to touch the sand with your club. In playing the shot, you tick the sand on your backswing, but you continue with your swing and execute a fine explosion shot. Since you did not improve your lie in the bunker, according to the Rules of Golf there is no need to call a penalty stroke on yourself. True or false?

False. It's a penalty whether or not you improve your lie.

114

"When in doubt, always call a woman Sugar." These sage words of advice were uttered by that formidable man of the world:

A. Walter Hagen, a man well worth listening to on many subjects.

B. Ike Grainger, the veteran USGA official. When he assumed the presidency of that organization, Grainger made a witty acceptance speech in which he first read the original 13 Rules of Golf and then appended 13 rules for running a successful women's tournament.

C. Dean Martin, in his welcoming address when the Los Angeles Open was moved to his club, Riviera.

D. Gerald Micklem, the colorful star of the Dominican Republic's Eisenhower Trophy team, who also heads up the Domino Sugar Company and never loses a chance to plug his product.

236 GOLF QUIZ

A. Hagen. It was one of his most typical confections.

115

All but one of the following statements about Bobby Jones' adventures enroute to the Grand Slam are correct. Which one is incorrect?

A. In the British Amateur, at St. Andrews, Jones had to go an extra hole to defeat Cyril Tolley, had to hole an eight-footer on the 18th to defeat Jimmy Johnston, and had to win three of the last five holes to edge George Voigt on the home green.

B. In the British Open, at Hoylake, Jones was sailing along smoothly on his last round until he made a double-bogey 7 on the eighth hole, a shortish par 5. From just off the edge of the green, it took him five shots to get down. This included missing a putt a foot long.

C. Jones eventually won our Open, at Minikahda, by two shots, but he had an erratic 76 on the fourth round and wasn't safely home until he birdied the last two holes.

D. Jones' victory in the U.S. Amateur, at Merion, which completed his Slam, was never really in doubt as he rolled over Ross Somerville, Fred Hoblitzel, Fay Coleman, Jess Sweetser and, finally, Eugene Homans.

C. The 1930 U.S. Open was held at Interlachen and not at Minikahda. Bobby also finished with a 75 and not a 76. He didn't birdie the last two holes. He birdied the 72nd but took a double bogey on the 71st.

116

The first man to shoot below his age in a PGA Tour tournament was

A. Gene Sarazen, who had a 68 in the Doral Open in 1971.

B. Harry Vardon, who had a 65 in the Asheville Open during his American tour in 1920.

C. Harry Cooper, who came out of retirement for the 1974 Texas Open and shot a blazing 67.

D. Sam Snead, who in 1979 posted a 66 on his final round in the Quad Cities Open.

240 GOLF QUIZ

D. Old Sam.

117 Who are Vicente, Baldomero and Manuel?

A. The brothers of Olin Dutra, the 1934 U.S. Open champion.

B. The brothers of Severiano Ballesteros, the 1979 British Open champion.

C. The brothers of Roberto de Vicenzo, the 1967 British Open champion.

D. The other three Dutch-owned Caribbean islands, which, along with Aruba, Bonaire and Curacao, are the sites of the annual Caribbean Duty Free Open.

B. They're the other Ballesteros boys.

118 So much has been said and written about Jack Nicklaus and his multiple accomplishments that many of us are now prone to forget some of the fundamentals of his approach to the game of golf. One of the following is correct.

A. Since his days as a junior golfer, he has been a natural right-to-left player.
B. Despite his great length off the tee, he drives—and has always driven—with a wood that has the loft of a brassie.
C. He grew up using a wooden-shafted putter, and still does.
D. He is one of the few modern champions who uses the interlocking grip.

244 GOLF QUIZ

D. Jack interlocks, always has.

119

You are engaged in an 18-hole battle at match play. On the seventh green your opponent's putt for a 3 finishes four inches from the cup. You leave it there, and your subsequent putt for a 3 caroms off that ball and into the cup. Your score for the hole is

A. 5. Under the rules of golf, in match play a golfer is assessed a two-stroke penalty if his ball strikes his opponent's ball.

B. 3. It is perfectly okay in match play to carom your ball off your opponent's when putting. No penalty.

C. Irrelevant. If your ball strikes your opponent's ball in match play, the penalty is loss of hole.

D. As Rule 74, Paragraph 3 clearly states, "Should a competitor, his partner, or one of their caddies strike an opponent's ball with his own or interfere with his stance or stroke, then, unless the flagstick has been removed or a provisional ball been put in play, the ball struck is deemed to be an immovable obstruction and, except if casual water obtains, the penalty for moving it is one stroke, provided no outside agency has rendered the ball unfit for play."

B. There is no penalty in match play if your ball strikes your opponent's ball on the green.

120

Take the number of courses at the Baltusrol Golf Club, the venue of the 1980 U.S. Open. Multiply this by the maximum number of clubs a player can carry in his bag. Add the record number of consecutive victories that Nancy Lopez scored during the 1978 LPGA season. Divide this by the record number of consecutive PGA Tour victories that Byron Nelson scored in 1945. Add the number of members of the Ryder family who were responsible for donating the Ryder Cup as the symbol of victory in the series of international matches. Your answer should be

- **A.** 2
- **B.** 5
- **C.** 7
- **D.** 4

248 GOLF QUIZ

D. 4. Baltusrol has two courses. Fourteen is the maximum number of clubs you can carry. Nancy won five straight tournaments. Byron won 11 straight. Samuel Ryder was the sole donor of the trophy that bears his name. 2 × 14 is 28. 28 plus 5 is 33. 33 divided by 11 is 3. 3 plus 1 is 4.